This book belongs to

_____

King Cake

Written by Brendon Oldendorf
Illustrated by Mary Ann McCall

ABCs

PELICAN PUBLISHING
NEW ORLEANS

The word "Pelican" and the depiction of a pelican are
trademarks of Arcadia Publishing Company Inc. and are
registered in the U.S. Patent and Trademark Office.

ISBN: 9781455627622

Printed in China
Published by Pelican Publishing
New Orleans, LA
www.pelicanpub.com

Brendon

Molly

Luke

Mason

Anna Grace

Brody

Hope

James

To all our family and friends who love king cake and especially our little king cake eaters carrying on the tradition. The best slice is the one with the baby!
—B.O. and M.M.

A

A is for
Ash Wednesday.

MARCH

✝ ASH

TUESDAY WEDNESDAY THURSDAY

Everything stops for a reason.
This is the day after king cake season.

B

B is for Baby.

Included for tradition, but not a mistake,
this baby is featured in every king cake.

1

C

C is for Colors.

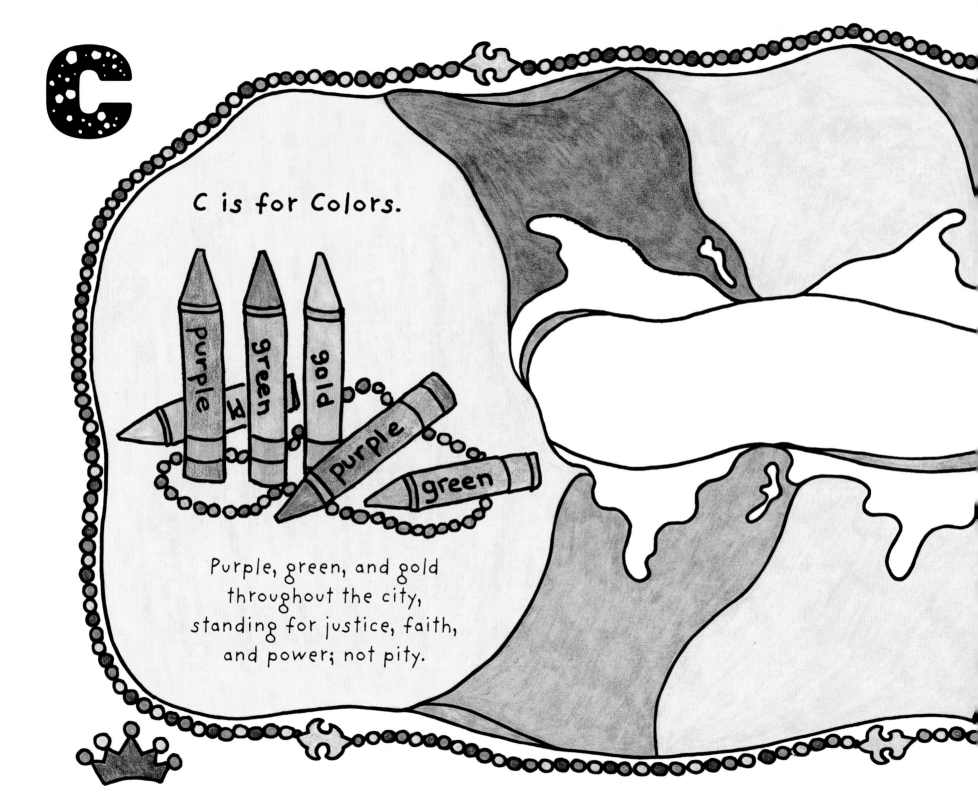

Purple, green, and gold
throughout the city,
standing for justice, faith,
and power; not pity.

D is for Dough.

Brioche with cinnamon and butter,
a taste like no other.

E is for Epiphany.

This day starts Carnival,
the season when the king cakes are
remarkable.

F is for Fat Tuesday.

The day of elation with no hesitation. The Crescent City's day of fascination.

G

G is for
Granulated Sugar.

A staple on the famous pastry,
which makes it really tasty.

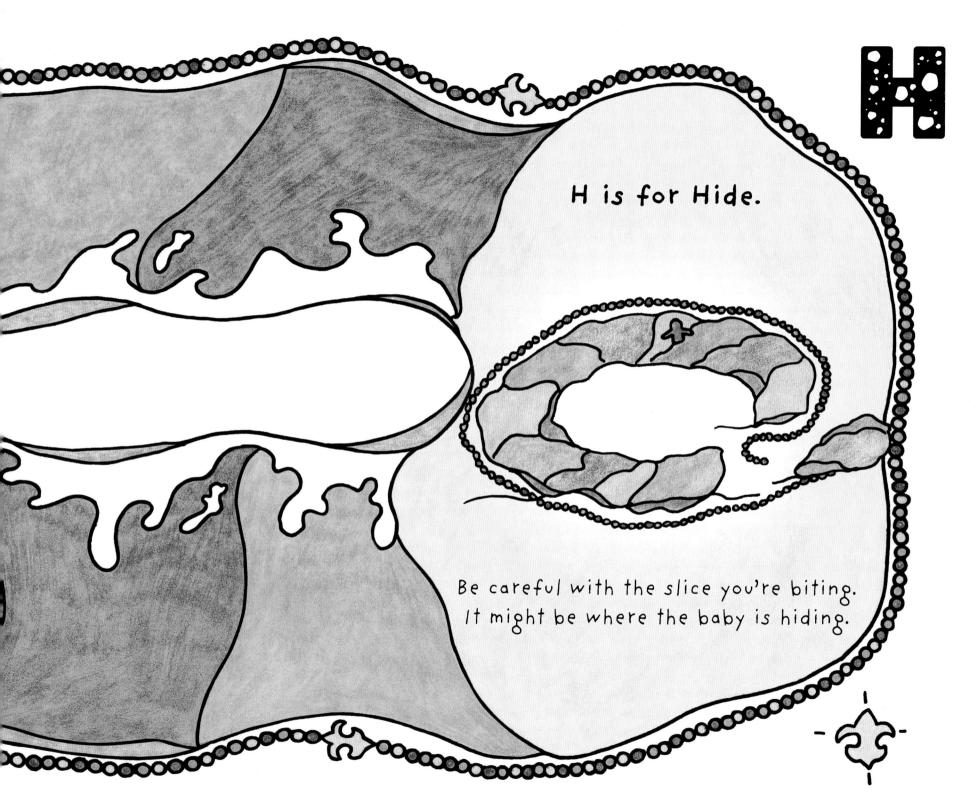

H is for Hide.

Be careful with the slice you're biting.
It might be where the baby is hiding.

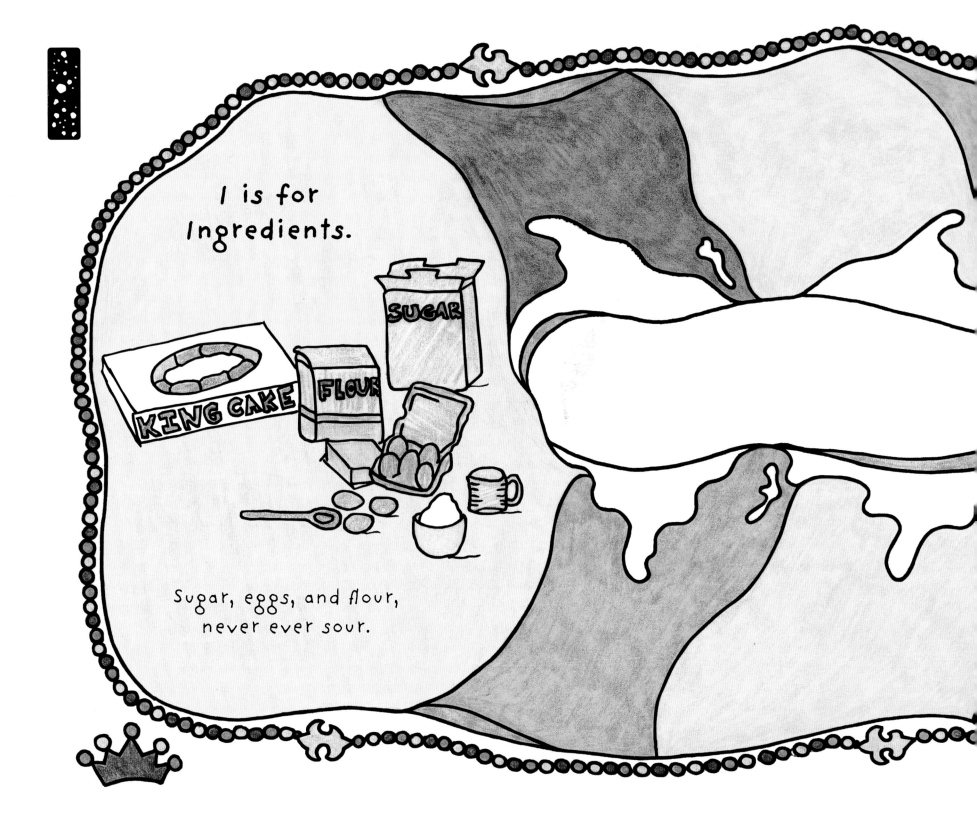

I is for
Ingredients.

Sugar, eggs, and flour,
never ever sour.

J is for Jesus.

"John 3:16"

It is not a mystery,
He is part of the history.

K is for King.

As head of the parade,
this royal has it made.

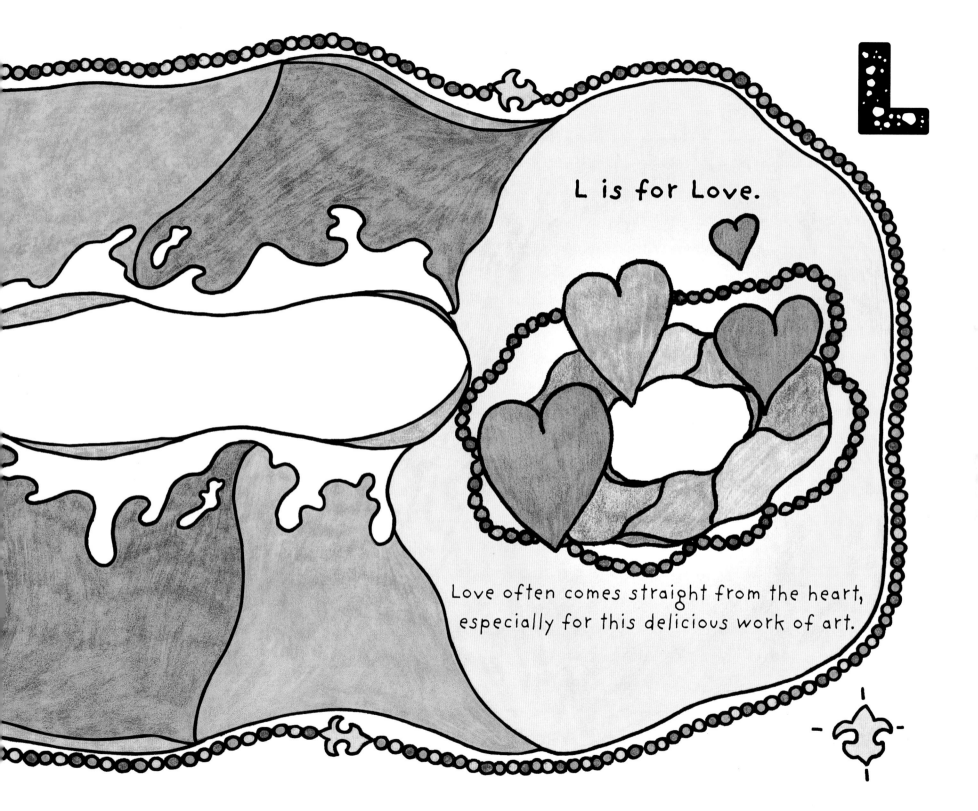

L is for Love.

Love often comes straight from the heart,
especially for this delicious work of art.

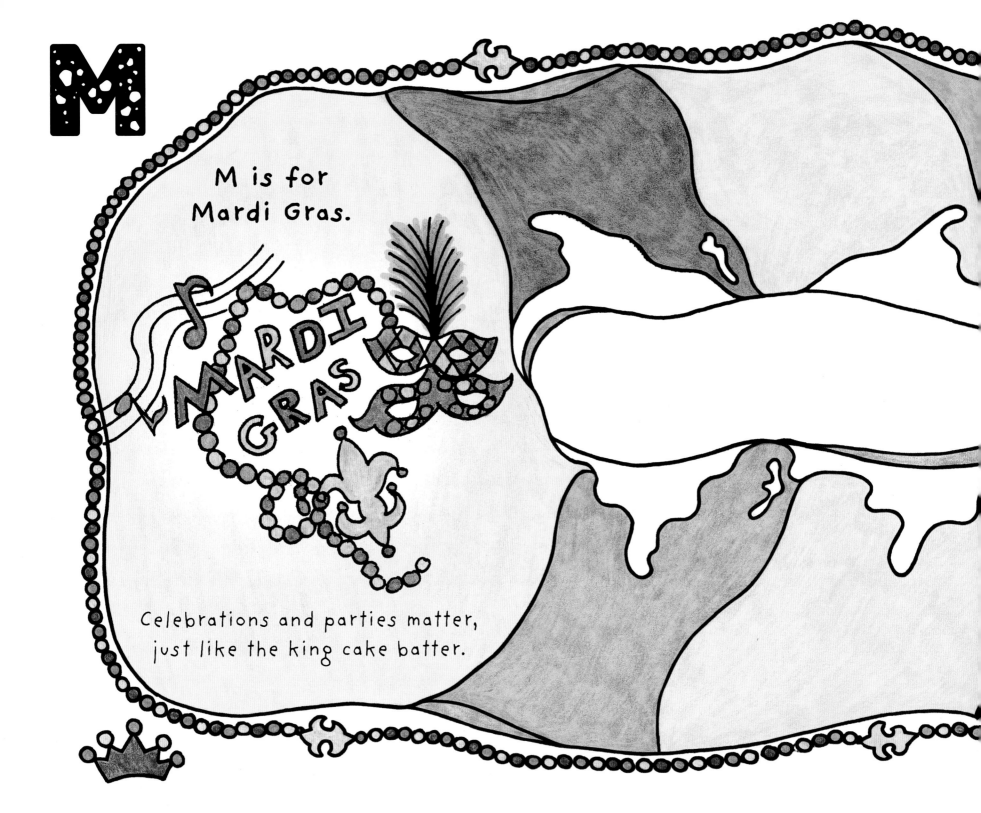

M

M is for
Mardi Gras.

MARDI GRAS

Celebrations and parties matter,
just like the king cake batter.

O

O is for Oval.

Most king cakes are circular,
but some are square.
Either way, they are made to share.

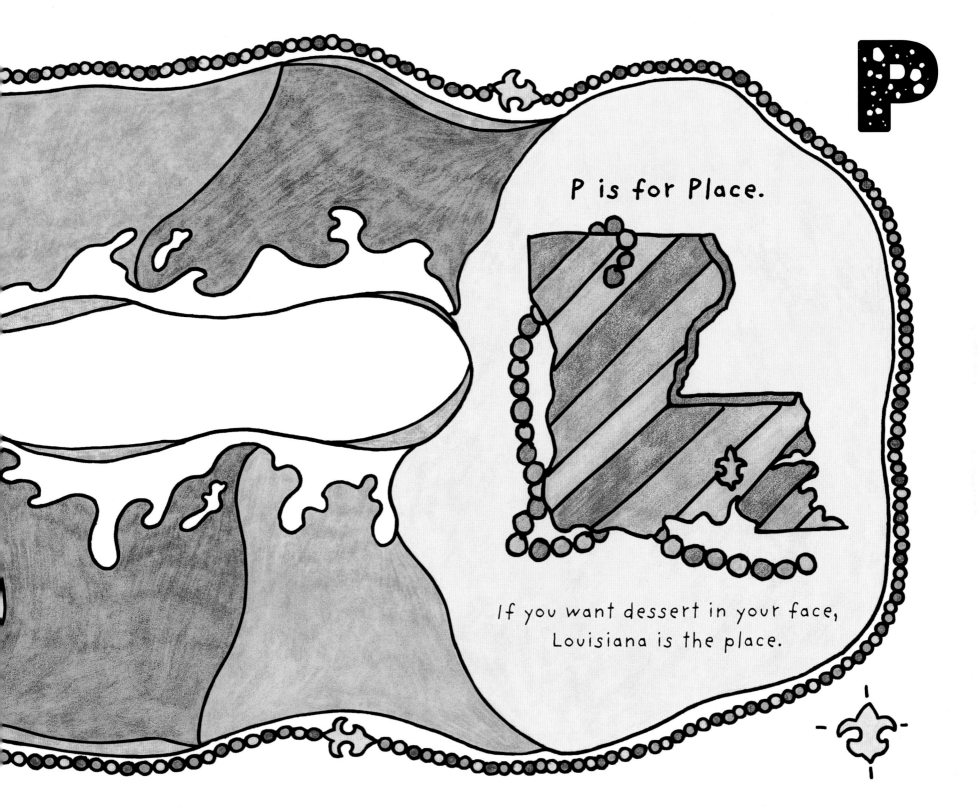

P is for Place.

If you want dessert in your face,
Louisiana is the place.

Q

Q is for Queen.

Just like the king,
but with more bling.

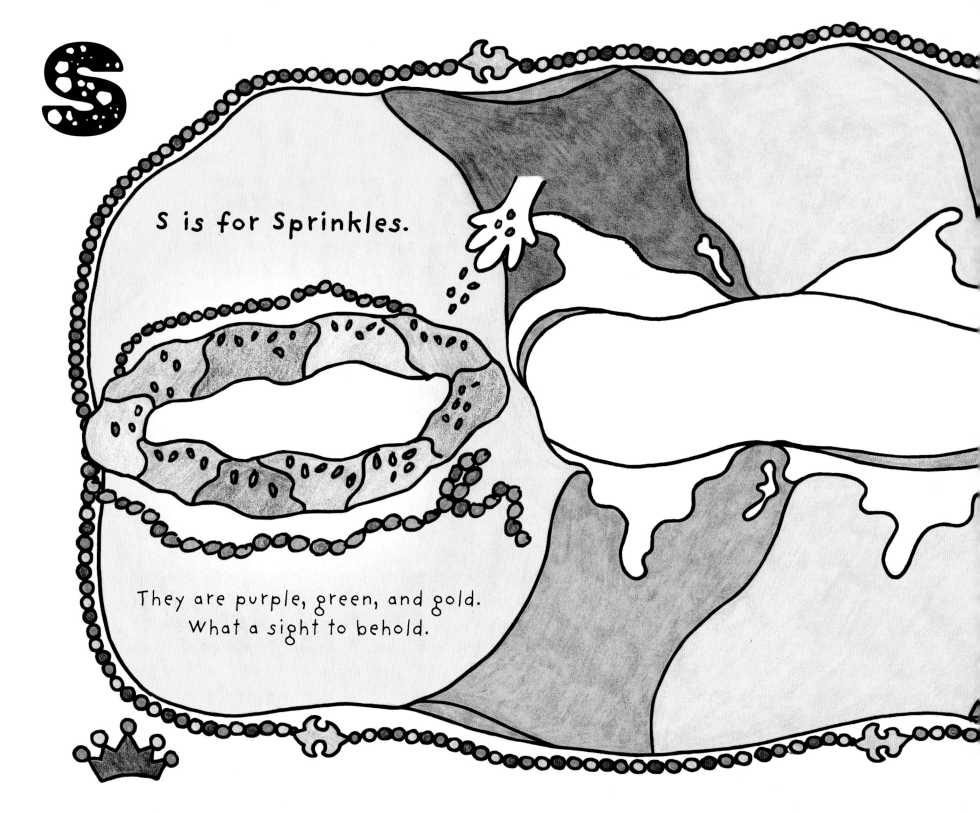

S is for Sprinkles.

They are purple, green, and gold.
What a sight to behold.

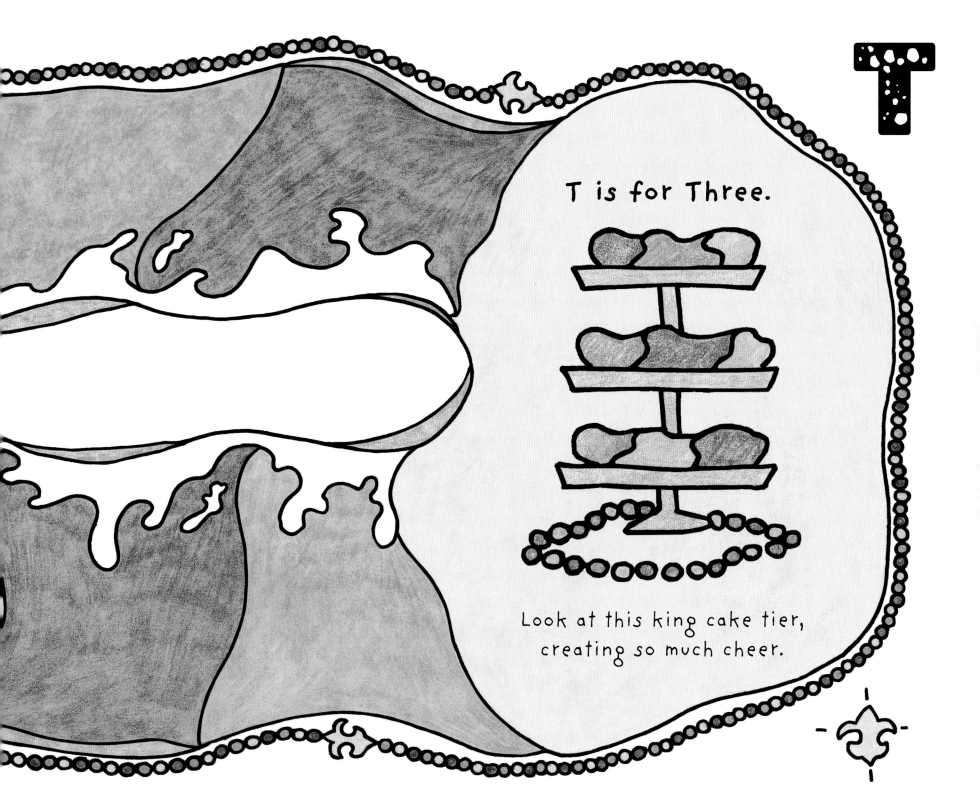

T is for Three.

Look at this king cake tier,
creating so much cheer.

U

U is for Unique.

Plain, filled, or savory,
received fresh from the bakery.

W is for
Wise Men.

These guys played a part,
and were also very smart.

X

X is for X-mas.

Just after this holiday,
king cake is the best entrée.

Y is for Yummy.

Most people can't get enough,
since it is made
with all the good stuff.

Z is for Zesty.

This savory king cake has some spice, as it is made with crawfish, pepper jelly, and rice.

Brendon Oldendorf, also known as the King Cake King, was born and raised in the *New Orleans Metro* area where he currently resides with his queen and their four young princes. He remembers his first king cake party as a child and enjoys having king cake parties to this day. A graduate of LSU in *Electrical Engineering*, Oldendorf currently works as a project manager for the local power company. When he is not working or parenting, he loves tasting and reviewing king cakes while posting humorous videos to the web. Check out www.kingcakeplanet. com for all his endeavors, which include him tasting 227 different king cakes from 151 bakeries during the 2023 Carnival season!

Mary Ann was born in Lafayette, LA and raised in *New Orleans*. She has always been a fan of king cake. She has worked for years teaching art to kids, and now she is happy to help her nephew illustrate his first king cake book. She wants to thank her husband, two daughters, two sons-in-law, three granddaughters, and one grandson for all their support and inspiration over the years!

Message from the King Cake King:

After reading this book, it is time for a quest:
tasting all the king cakes to determine the best.
Make sure it's January sixth before you begin,
as king cake mania will start again.
Come for a visit along the gulf coast,
or have your king cake shipped for a toast.
Next day delivery right to your door,
traditional or filled makes you want more.
Be sure to share with everyone around,
taking note of where the baby was found.
Whoever it was will be king for the day,
tis the tradition you must portray.
The season is less than a quarter of the year,
eat as many as you can, delighting in cheer.
I hope you build on this delicious foundation,
as it has given me a lot of inspiration.

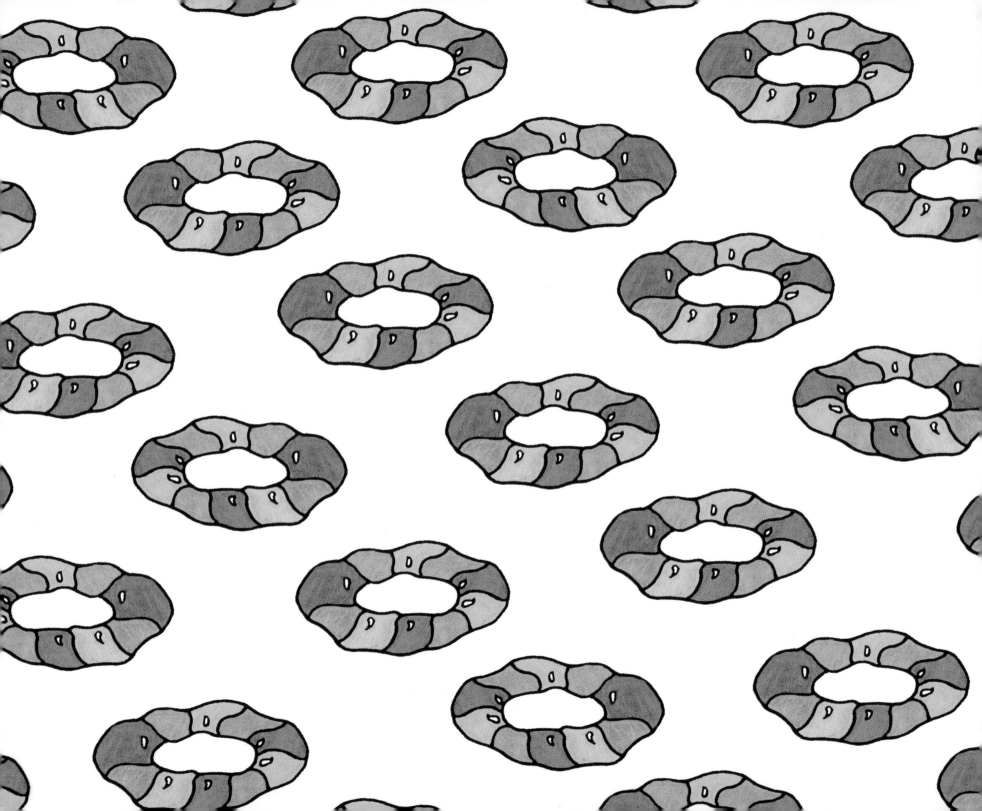